*Christianity*
E✟PLORED
UNIVERSAL

One life. Pure and simple.

Christianity Explored Universal Handbook (2nd Edition)
Copyright © 2012 Christianity Explored / The Good Book Company
www.ceministries.org

Published by
The Good Book Company
Tel (UK): 0333 123 0880
Tel (Int) +44 (0) 208 942 0880
Email: admin@thegoodbook.co.uk

Websites
UK & Europe: www.thegoodbook.co.uk
North America: www.thegoodbook.com
Australia: www.thegoodbook.com.au
New Zealand: www.thegoodbook.co.nz

ISBN 9781908317889

CHRISTIANITY
E✝PLORED
MINISTRIES

thegoodbook
COMPANY

In the UK such licences are issued by the Copyright Licensing
Agency, 90 Tottenham Court Road, London W1P 9HE. BRITISH
LIBRARY CATALOGUING IN PUBLICATION DATA. A catalogue
record for this book is available from the British Library.

Unless otherwise stated, Scripture quotations are taken from the
HOLY BIBLE, NEW INTERNATIONAL VERSION Copyright © 1973,
1978, 1984 by the International Bible Society.

Used by permission of Hodder and Stoughton Limited. All rights
reserved.

Grateful thanks to: Barry Cooper, Craig Dyer, Alison Mitchell,
Stephen Nichols, Sam Shammas, Rico Tice, Tim Thornborough,
Nicole Wagner Carter, Su Ann Woo and Anne Woodcock, and the
many others who contributed to the development of the Christianity
Explored Universal Edition.

Design by Steve Devane and André Parker

Printed in China

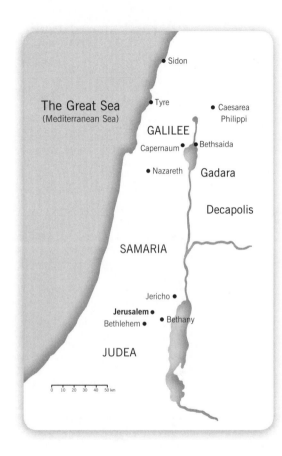

The Great Sea
(Mediterranean Sea)

Sidon

Tyre

Caesarea
Philippi

GALILEE

Capernaum • Bethsaida

Nazareth

Gadara

Decapolis

SAMARIA

Jericho

Jerusalem • Bethany
Bethlehem

JUDEA

0  10  20  30  40  50 km

## Before we begin

Over the next eight sessions we will explore Christianity by seeing what the Bible has to say about Jesus Christ. In particular, we will explore three questions about Jesus:

• Who is he?
• Why did he come?
• What does it mean to follow him?

The Bible contains 66 books. Many human authors wrote these books over 1500 years. God's Holy Spirit inspired each author. This means that when we read the Bible, we are reading God's words — exactly what he wants us to know.

The Bible is divided into two main sections: the Old Testament and the New Testament. The Old Testament was written before Jesus was born and the New Testament was written after Jesus was born.

In this course we will read the book of Mark (also known as Mark's Gospel), which is a historical account of Jesus' life. Mark's Gospel is divided up into chapters and each chapter is divided into individual verses, all of which are numbered. So **Mark 1:1 – 3:6** refers to the book of Mark, chapter 1, verse 1, through to chapter 3, verse 6. All the Bible references in this handbook are written in this way.

During the course we will study various passages from Mark's Gospel. You may also ask any questions about Christianity, no matter how simple or difficult you think they are.

# What is Christianity?

■ If you could ask God one question, and you knew it would be answered, what would it be?

_____

_____

_____

■ What do many people think Christianity is about?

☐ Christianity is about being a good person

☐ Christianity is about going to church

☐ Christianity is a western religion

☐ Christianity is about following the teachings of Jesus Christ

☐ Christianity is _____

*Christianity Explored* takes us through the Gospel of Mark so that we can discover the real answer to the question: "What is Christianity?"

---

**WHO WAS MARK?**

Mark was a friend and companion of Peter, who was one of Jesus' closest friends. Peter was an "apostle", someone chosen to tell other people about the life, death and resurrection (rising from death) of Jesus.

Peter wrote two of the letters in the Bible (known as 1 and 2 Peter). In his second letter he said: *"I will make every effort to see that after my departure* (death) *you will always remember these things"* (2 Peter 1:15). He meant the things he saw and knew about Jesus. He passed them on to others like Mark.

Peter died about 30 years after Jesus died. The evidence tells us that Mark wrote his book around then. Mark's Gospel is one of four books in the Bible telling the life story of Jesus. The others were written by Matthew, Luke and John.

*Are there any words you do not understand?*
*Look at the Bible words list to help you.*

**1** What do we learn about Christianity from this verse?

_____

_____

_____

**2** Some people criticise Christianity. They say:

"It is a list of rules."

"It is about going to church and pretending to be a good person."

"It is boring."

How does Mark answer these criticisms in Mark 1:1?

_____

_____

_____

**BIBLE WORDS**

**Mark 1:1**

**v1 gospel.** Good news.

**v1 Christ/Messiah.** God's only chosen King, who God promised to send into the world.

6

*Are there any words you do not understand?*
*Look at the Bible words list to help you.*

Jesus was baptized by John in the Jordan river. As Jesus came up out of the water, God the Holy Spirit came down on him in the form of a dove, and God the Father spoke.

**3** What did God the Father say about Jesus?

_____

_____

_____

**4** Is there anything that surprises, interests or puzzles you about Jesus?

_____

_____

_____

## Summary

Christianity is the good news (the "gospel") about Jesus Christ.

Mark tells us that Jesus is God's chosen King, known as the Christ or Messiah. Mark also shows that Jesus is the Son of God.

### BIBLE WORDS

**Mark 1:9–11**

**v9 Nazareth.** A town in the north of the country of Israel. Jesus grew up in Nazareth. See map on page 4.

**v9 Galilee.** The northern area of the country of Israel. See map on page 4.

**v9 baptized.** John baptized people in the Jordan river by dipping them under the water. Baptism is a symbol or picture of turning away from sin and being washed clean on the inside.

**v10 Spirit.** The Holy Spirit. The Bible teaches that there is one God in three persons: God the Father, God the Son (that's Jesus) and God the Holy Spirit.

# Who is Jesus?

■ **Who do your friends or family think Jesus is?**

☐ A good teacher

☐ A prophet

☐ A political leader

☐ The Son of God

☐ Other _____

**Read aloud Mark 2:1–12**

*Are there any words you do not understand?*
*Look at the Bible words list on the next two pages to help you.*

**1** What problem did the four men have (see verses 2-4)?

_____

_____

---

**THE STORY SO FAR**

◁ Christianity is about Jesus Christ.

◁ It is the good news (the "gospel") about Jesus.

◁ When Jesus was baptized by John, God's voice was heard. God called Jesus his Son.

**2** How did the four men solve this problem (see verse 4)?

_____

_____

**3** What did they expect Jesus to do for the paralyzed man?

_____

_____

**4** What did Jesus do (see verse 5)? Why do you think he did that?

_____

_____

_____

**5** Why were the religious leaders so angry (see verses 6-7)?

_____

_____

_____

## BIBLE WORDS

**Mark 2:1–12**

**v1 Capernaum.** A town near the Sea of Galilee. See map on page 4.

**v2 gathered.** Came together in a group.

**v2 preached the word.** Taught people the good news (the "gospel").

**v3 paralytic.** A person who is unable to move their legs and maybe their arms as well.

**v5 faith.** Trust/belief. Faith in God means trusting that God will do what he says.

**v5 sins.** Rebellion against God; doing what _we_ want instead of what _God_ wants.

**v5 forgiven.** Treated as if we had never sinned.

**v6 teachers of the law.** Jewish religious leaders. Teachers of the Jewish religious law.

**v6 blaspheming.** Lying about God, or claiming to have rights and powers that belong to God.

**6** Look at the question Jesus asks in verse 9. How would you answer it? Why?

_____

_____

_____

**7** Why did Jesus heal the man (see verses 10-12)?

_____

_____

_____

In Mark 2:10 Jesus calls himself the "Son of Man". The prophet Daniel came from Israel 500 years before Mark. He described the son of man:

_"In my vision at night I looked, and there before me was one like a son of man, coming with the clouds of heaven … He was given authority, glory and sovereign power; all peoples, nations and men of every language worshipped him."_ (Daniel 7:13-14)

**8** In your own words, how did Daniel describe the son of man?

_____

_____

_____

**9** Daniel's book was well known in Israel. What did Jesus expect people to understand when he called himself the "Son of Man" in Mark 2:10?

_____

_____

_____

**10** What does this event tell us about who Jesus is?

_____

_____

## Summary

Jesus has power and authority to forgive sin.

Mark also shows that Jesus has power and authority:

- to teach (see for example Mark 1:21-22)

- over evil spirits (see for example Mark 1:23-27)

- over sickness (see for example Mark 1:29-34)

- over nature (see for example Mark 4:35-41)

- and even over death (see for example Mark 5:35-42)

The evidence in Mark's Gospel tells us that Jesus was a man with the power and authority of God himself. He is the Son of God.

# Why did Jesus come?

## THE STORY SO FAR

◁ Christianity is about Jesus Christ.

◁ It is the good news (the "gospel") about Jesus.

◁ When Jesus was baptized by John, God's voice was heard. God called Jesus his Son.

◁ When four men brought a paralyzed man to Jesus, he forgave the man's sin. Then Jesus healed the man to prove that he has the power and authority to forgive sin.

◁ Mark's Gospel shows that Jesus has the power and authority of God himself. Jesus is the Son of God.

■ **What do you think is the world's biggest problem?**

☐ War

☐ Poverty

☐ Pollution

☐ Racism

☐ Greed

☐ Other _____

■ **In our last session, what was the paralyzed man's biggest problem?**

_____

_____

_____

*Read the verses again. Are there any words you do not understand?*
*Look at the Bible words list to help you.*

**1** How should we treat God (see verse 30)?

_____

_____

**2** How do we treat God?

_____

_____

None of us has loved God as we should. Instead of loving God, we have all turned away from him.

We have all rebelled against God by doing what *we* want instead of what *he* wants. This is called sin.

**Read Mark 7:20–23**

**3** Where does sin come from (see verses 21 and 23)?

_____

_____

**Mark 12:28–30**

**v28 teachers of the law.** A group of Jewish religious leaders.

**v28 debating.** Discussing, arguing.

**v28 commandments.** Instructions, rules. The "Ten Commandments" were given by God to show his rescued people how to live.

**v29 "Hear, O Israel".** A command telling the Israelites to listen to God.

**v29 Lord.** Master or leader.

**v30 heart, soul, mind, strength.** Every part of you.

**Mark 7:20–23**

**v20 unclean.** Dirty in God's sight. If someone was "unclean", they could not enter the temple in Jerusalem.

**v21 sexual immorality.** Any sexual thoughts or actions that are not part of marriage.

**v21 adultery.** Sex with a person who is married to someone else.

**v22 malice.** Doing something to deliberately harm someone else.

**4** What is the result of our sin (see verses 20 and 23)?

_____

_____

_____

The evils that come out of our hearts make us "unclean". They keep us away from God because he is completely pure and good.

God will not ignore our sin – it must be punished.

Sin is our greatest problem.

**Read aloud Mark 9:43–47**

**5** What does Jesus tell us to do about the causes of sin?

_____

_____

**6** Why do you think Jesus uses such serious examples when talking about the need to avoid hell?

_____

_____

_____

## BIBLE WORDS

**v22 deceit.** Cheating, lying.

**v22 lewdness.** Being crude about sexual things.

**v22 envy.** Wanting what belongs to other people.

**v22 slander.** Telling lies about someone.

**v22 arrogance.** Pride. Thinking you are better or more clever than others.

**v22 folly.** Foolishness.

**Mark 9:43–47**

**v43 causes you to.** Makes you.

**v43 sin.** Doing what _we_ want instead of what _God_ wants. Sin is rebellion against God.

**v43 maimed.** Permanently injured.

**v44 hell.** Being separated from God, and from everything that is good, for ever.

**v44 crippled.** Disabled.

**v47 pluck.** Pull or pick out.

**v47 the kingdom of God.** God's kingdom isn't a place. It is God's people living with him as their King now and for ever.

**7** Jesus believed in hell. Should we? Why or why not?

_____

_____

**8** What would you say if someone said to you:
   "When I die, God will be pleased with me because I am a good person"?

_____

_____

_____

## Summary

• We have all sinned – we have rebelled against God.

• We are all unclean – we face his punishment.

• We all need to be forgiven – we need to be rescued.

That is why Jesus came.

Jesus said: "It is not the healthy who need a doctor, but the sick. I have not come to call the righteous, but sinners" (Mark 2:17).

Jesus came to rescue us from hell, the punishment our sin deserves, and to bring us into his kingdom. In the next session we will learn how he does that.

# Why did Jesus die?

Session 4

■ **Where do you see crosses today?**

_____

_____

In Jesus' day, people were punished by being nailed to a wooden cross and left to die. It was terrible and shameful to die in this way.

God spoke about this kind of punishment hundreds of years before when he said: "Anyone who is hung on a tree is under God's curse" (Deuteronomy 21:23).

Mark's Gospel tells us that Jesus predicted his own death three times (Mark 8:31, 9:30-31, 10:32-34). He said that this "must" happen.

**Read aloud Mark 15:33–39**

_Read the verses again. Are there any words you do not understand?_
_Look at the Bible words list on the next page to help you._

**1 Read verse 33.** What unusual event happened at mid-day (the "sixth hour") as Jesus was dying?

_____

**THE STORY SO FAR**

◁ Christianity is about Jesus Christ. It is the good news (the "gospel") about Jesus.

◁ Jesus is the Son of God. He has the power and authority of God himself. This includes the power and authority to forgive sin.

◁ We have all sinned – we have rebelled against God.

◁ We all face God's punishment. We all need to be forgiven – we need to be rescued.

◁ Jesus came to rescue us from hell, the punishment our sin deserves.

**2** In the Bible, darkness is a sign of God's anger and judgment.
What is surprising about the focus of God's anger here?

_____

_____

God punished Jesus, so that we don't have to be punished.

**3** What was the relationship between Jesus and his Father before his death on the cross?
(See Mark 1:9-11 and Mark 9:7.)

_____

_____

**4 Read verse 34.** What happened between Jesus and his Father at the cross?

_____

_____

Jesus chose to be abandoned so that we do not have to be.

**5 Read verses 37–38.** What happened in the temple in Jerusalem when Jesus died?

_____

_____

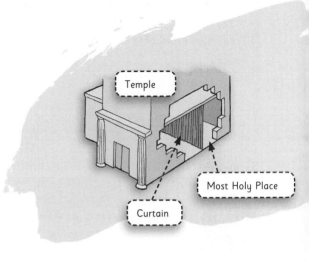

Temple

Most Holy Place

Curtain

Sinful people cannot meet with God, because he is holy.

The curtain in the middle of the temple stopped sinful people from meeting with God in the Most Holy Place (see picture).

Only once a year, a priest was able to go through the curtain and meet with God in the Most Holy Place. But the priest could only do that after he made special sacrifices.

**6** How did Jesus' death change our relationship with God?

_____

_____

We can be accepted by God because Jesus died for us. The way to God is now open.

**Read Mark 10:45**

**7** Why did Jesus die?

_____

_____

**BIBLE WORDS**

**Mark 10:45**

**v45 the Son of Man.** A title (name) Jesus often used about himself.

**v45 ransom.** A price paid to buy back and/or free a slave.

Jesus died in our place to pay the price – the ransom – for our sin.

**8** What is your reaction to this?

_____

_____

_____

## Summary

Jesus was punished – instead of us.

Jesus chose to be abandoned – so that we do not have to be.

Jesus died as a ransom – to pay the price for our sin.

As Jesus died, the curtain in the temple was torn in two from top to bottom.
This shows that we can be accepted by God because Jesus died for us.
The way to God is now open.

# Why did Jesus rise from the dead?

■ **What do you think happens to us after we die?**

_____

_____

**Read aloud Mark 15:42–47**

*Read the verses again. Are there any words you do not understand?*
*Look at the Bible words list on the next page to help you.*

**1** How did Pilate, the Roman governor, know that Jesus was dead (see verses 44-45)?

_____

_____

**2** Where was Jesus buried (see verse 46)?

_____

_____

---

**THE STORY SO FAR**

◁ Christianity is about Jesus Christ. It is the good news (the "gospel") about Jesus.

◁ Jesus is the Son of God. He has the power and authority of God himself. This includes the power and authority to forgive sin.

◁ We have all sinned – we have rebelled against God.

◁ We all face God's punishment. We all need to be forgiven – we need to be rescued.

◁ Jesus came to rescue us from hell, the punishment our sin deserves.

◁ God punished Jesus so that we don't have to be punished. Jesus died on a cross as a ransom, to pay the price for our sin.

◁ We can be accepted by God because Jesus died for us.

**3** Why did the women go to Jesus' tomb (see verse 1)?

_____

_____

**4** What were they thinking about as they went to the tomb (see verses 2-3)?

_____

_____

**5** What did they find when they got to the tomb (see verses 4-6)?

_____

_____

**6** The empty tomb should not have surprised the women. Why not?
(See verse 7 and Mark 14:28.)

_____

_____

Jesus told his followers that he would rise from the dead. He said they would see him again.

## BIBLE WORDS

**Mark 15:42–47**

**v42 Preparation Day.** The day before the Sabbath.

**v42 Sabbath.** Jewish holy day. The Sabbath lasts from sunset on Friday to sunset on Saturday.

**v42 approached.** Came near.

**v43 Arimathea.** A town in the south of Israel.

**v43 prominent.** Important.

**v43 the Council.** Important group of Jewish leaders.

**v43 waiting for the kingdom of God.** Waiting for God to send his chosen King to lead his people.

**v43 boldly.** Bravely.

**v43 Pilate.** The Roman governor in charge of Israel.

**v44 summoning.** Sending for.

**v45 centurion.** Roman army officer.

**v46 linen.** Type of material/cloth.

**v46 tomb.** Cave cut out of the rocky hillside to bury a body in.

**v46 entrance.** Way in, opening.

**7** In the following verses what did Jesus say he came to do?

• Mark 8:31

_____

_____

• Mark 9:30-31

_____

_____

• Mark 10:32-34

_____

_____

Jesus said he would suffer, be rejected and die. Three times Jesus said he would rise from the dead.

**8** Why did Jesus have to die and rise again? (See Mark 10:45.)

_____

_____

_____

**BIBLE WORDS**

**Mark 16:1–8**

**v1 anoint Jesus' body.** Put oil or spices on the body of Jesus.

**v2 first day of the week.** Sunday.

**v5 robe.** Long piece of clothing.

**v5 alarmed.** Scared, frightened.

**v6 Nazarene.** Someone from Nazareth, a town in the north of Israel (see map on page 4).

**v6 crucified.** Nailed to a cross and left to die.

**v6 risen.** Come to life again.

**v6 laid him.** Put him down.

**v7 disciples.** Followers.

**v7 Galilee.** The north part of Israel. See map on page 4.

**v8 trembling.** Shaking.

**v8 bewildered.** Puzzled, confused.

**v8 fled.** Ran away.

**9** What does the resurrection (rising from death) show us about Jesus?

_____

_____

_____

## Summary

Jesus died and was buried in a tomb cut out of rock.
He died to pay the price for our sin. Jesus took the punishment we deserve.

Two days after he died, Jesus rose from the dead, just as he said he would.
His resurrection shows that he has power and authority over death
— not just over his own death, but over ours as well.

Jesus died and rose again.
We know from the rest of the Bible that Christians will also die and rise again.
Everyone who puts their trust in Jesus will rise again to be with God for ever.

# How can God accept us?

■ If you died today, why should God give you eternal life?

_____

_____

_____

_____

**Read aloud Mark 10:17–22**

*Read the verses again. Are there any words you do not understand?*
*Look at the Bible words list on the next page to help you.*

**1** What did the rich man want to know (see verse 17)?

_____

_____

_____

**THE STORY SO FAR**

◀ Christianity is about Jesus Christ. It is the good news (the "gospel") about Jesus.

◀ Jesus is the Son of God. He has the power and authority of God himself.

◀ We have all sinned. We all face God's punishment. We all need to be forgiven.

◀ Jesus came to rescue us from hell, the punishment our sin deserves.

◀ God punished Jesus for our sin. Jesus died on a cross as a ransom, to pay the price for our sin.

◀ Jesus rose from the dead, just as he said he would.

◀ Everyone who puts their trust in Jesus will rise again to be with God for ever.

**2** What commandments did the man say he had kept (see verses 19-20)?

_____

_____

_____

**Read Mark 12:28–30**

**3** What did Jesus say was the most important commandment (see verses 29-30)?

_____

_____

_____

Jesus said we must love God with every part of our lives.

**4** What did Jesus say the rich man should do (see Mark 10:21)?
The man thought that he loved God. How did this show him that he did not love God with every part of his life (see Mark 10:22)?

_____

_____

_____

---

**BIBLE WORDS**

**Mark 10:17–22**

**v17 inherit.** Receive, be given. A person may inherit something when a member of their family dies.

**v17 eternal life.** Life with God both now and for ever.

**v19 commandments.** Instructions, rules. The "Ten Commandments" were given by God to show his rescued people how to live.

**v19 commit adultery.** Have sex with a person who is married to someone else.

**v19 give false testimony.** Tell lies about someone.

**v19 defraud.** Cheat someone to steal their money.

**v19 honour.** Respect.

**v21 lack.** Do not have.

**v22 the man's face fell.** He looked sad and unhappy.

**v22 wealth.** Riches, a lot of money.

**5** The man loved being rich more than he loved God.

What other things do people love more than God?

_____

_____

None of us deserves eternal life because none of us has loved God as we should.

**Read Mark 10:13–16**

**6** What did the children need to do in order to belong to the kingdom of God?

_____

_____

**7** How can anyone enter the kingdom of God (see verse 15)?

_____

_____

_____

The only way to enter the kingdom of God is to come to Jesus like a little child. We cannot earn eternal life. It is a free gift for everyone who comes to Jesus and puts their trust in him. The Bible calls this grace.

**BIBLE WORDS**

**Mark 12:28–30**

**v28 teachers of the law.** A group of Jewish religious leaders.

**v28 debating.** Discussing, arguing.

**v29 "Hear, O Israel".** A command telling the Israelites to listen to God.

**v30 heart, soul, mind, strength.** Every part of you.

**Mark 10:13–16**

**v13 rebuked.** Strongly criticised, told off.

**v14 indignant.** Angry.

**v14 hinder.** Prevent, stop.

**v14 the kingdom of God.** God's kingdom is not a place. It is God's people living with him as their King now and for ever.

**v14 such as these.** People like these children.

**v15 receive.** Accept.

**v16 blessed them.** Prayed for them.

**8** What is wrong with the man's question in Mark 10:17?

_____

_____

_____

## Summary

We are all like the man in Mark 10.
We do not love God with every part of our lives.

We deserve to be punished.

But God the Father loves us so much that he sent his Son to rescue us.
Jesus died to pay the price for our sin.

We cannot earn God's forgiveness and eternal life by doing good things.
God gives us the gift of forgiveness and eternal life if we put our trust
in Jesus Christ.

This is what grace is – a gift from God that we don't deserve and cannot earn.
God will accept everyone who comes to Jesus and puts their trust in him.

# What does it mean to follow Jesus?

◼ **What do you think when you hear the word "Christian"?**

_____

_____

_____

**Read aloud Mark 8:27–30**

*Read the verses again. Are there any words you do not understand?*
*Look at the Bible words list on the next page to help you.*

**1** What did Jesus ask his disciples in verse 27?

_____

**2** In verse 28, who did most people say Jesus was?

_____

_____

### THE STORY SO FAR

◁ Christianity is the good news (the "gospel") about Jesus Christ.

◁ Jesus is the Son of God. He has the power and authority of God himself.

◁ We have all sinned. We all face God's punishment. We all need to be forgiven.

◁ Jesus came to rescue us from hell, the punishment our sin deserves.

◁ God punished Jesus for our sin. Jesus died on a cross as a ransom, to pay the price for our sin.

◁ Jesus rose from the dead, just as he said he would.

◁ We cannot earn eternal life by doing good things.

◁ God gives us the gift of forgiveness and eternal life if we put our trust in Jesus Christ.

**3** Peter answered Jesus' question correctly. Who did he say Jesus is (see verse 29)?

_____

**4** How would you answer the question Jesus asked in verse 29?

_____

_____

**Read Mark 8:31–33**

"Christ" is a title. It means "God's chosen King". Jesus is the King who came to bring people into God's kingdom.

**5** The people of Israel were expecting the Christ to come and save them from their enemies. What did Jesus say he had come to do (see verse 31)?

_____

_____

_____

**6** How did Peter react to what Jesus said (see verse 32)?

_____

_____

## BIBLE WORDS

**Mark 8:27–38**

**v27 disciples.** Jesus' twelve closest friends.

**v27 Caesarea Philippi.** A town in the north of Israel. See the map on page 4.

**v28 John the Baptist.** A prophet. John baptized people (by dipping them under water) to show that they wanted to be washed clean of their sins by God.

**v28 Elijah.** An important prophet from the Old Testament part of the Bible.

**v28 prophets.** Messengers from God.

**v29 Christ.** A Greek word that means "God's chosen King". The same word in the Hebrew language is "Messiah".

**v31 the Son of Man.** A title (name) Jesus often used about himself.

**v31 elders, chief priests and teachers of the law.** Three groups of Jewish religious leaders.

**v31 rise again.** Come back to life.

**7** Why did Peter react like this (see verse 33)?

_____

_____

God the Father had a plan for his Son, Jesus Christ.
God's plan was very different from what Peter expected.

**8** Think about what you have already learned from Mark's Gospel.
Why did Jesus have to be killed and rise again?

_____

_____

Read Mark 8:34–38

**9** What did Jesus say that following him would mean (see verse 34)?

_____

_____

**10** Why is it wise to follow Jesus (see verses 35-38)?

_____

_____

_____

**BIBLE WORDS**

**v32 plainly.** Clearly.

**v32 aside.** To one side.

**v32 rebuke.** Criticise strongly.

**v33 Satan.** The devil.

**v33 the things of God.** What God says is good and important.

**v33 the things of men.** What people want, or think should be important.

**v34 come after me.** Follow me.

**v34 deny himself.** Not live for himself.

**v34 take up his cross.** Be ready to suffer (as Jesus suffered on the cross).

**v35 the gospel.** The good news about Jesus.

**v36 forfeit.** Lose.

**v36 soul.** Spirit.

**v38 adulterous and sinful generation.** People who have turned away from God.

**v38 comes in his Father's glory with the holy angels.** Comes from heaven as God's chosen, glorious King.

**11** In what ways would you have to deny yourself to follow Jesus?

_____

_____

**12** From what you have learned in Mark 8, describe what a Christian is.
Use your own words.

_____

_____

**13** Would you use the words above to describe yourself?

_____

_____

**Summary**

Jesus is the Christ – God's chosen King.

Jesus came to die – to pay the price for our sin.
He rose from the dead – just as he said he would.

Following Jesus means "denying ourselves" – no longer living for
ourselves but for Jesus. "Taking up our cross" means being prepared
to follow Jesus, whatever the cost.

# What next?

■ **Read "The story so far" on this page. Is there anything you do not understand?**

_____

_____

_____

**Read aloud Mark 4:1–9 and 4:13–20**

*Read the verses again. Are there any words you do not understand?*
*Look at the Bible words list on the next two pages to help you.*

Jesus often taught people by telling parables. A parable is a story with a deeper, sometimes hidden, meaning. In verses 3-8 Jesus tells the story. In verses 13-20 he explains what it means.

**1** What is the "seed" in this parable? (See verses 3 and 14.)

_____

_____

### THE STORY SO FAR

◁ Christianity is the good news (the "gospel") about Jesus Christ, the Son of God.

◁ We have all sinned. We all face God's punishment. We all need to be forgiven.

◁ Jesus came to rescue us from hell, the punishment our sin deserves.

◁ God punished Jesus for our sin. Jesus died on a cross to pay the price for our sin.

◁ Jesus rose from the dead, just as he said he would.

◁ We cannot earn eternal life by doing good things.

◁ God gives us the gift of forgiveness and eternal life if we put our trust in Jesus Christ.

◁ Following Jesus means "denying ourselves" and "taking up our cross".

**2** What happens when people hear God's word in verses 4 and 15?

_____

_____

The path is like people who hear the good news about Jesus, but "Satan comes and takes away the word" (Mark 4:15).

They hear about Jesus but quickly forget what they have heard.

**3** What happens when people hear God's word in verses 5-6 and 16-17?

_____

_____

**4** What does it mean that this kind of person who hears God's word "has no root"?

_____

_____

_____

The rocky soil is like those who are happy about what they hear, but "they last only a short time" (Mark 4:16-17).

When trouble comes as a result of following Jesus, they stop following him.

**BIBLE WORDS**

**Mark 4:1–9**

**v1 gathered.** Came together.

**v1 shore.** Beach, side of the lake.

**v2 parables.** Stories with a deeper meaning.

**v3 sow.** Spread seed, plant.

**v4 scattering.** Throwing, spreading.

**v5 sprang up.** Grew.

**v5 shallow.** Not deep.

**v6 scorched.** Burned.

**v6 withered.** Became weak and small.

**v7 choked.** Strangled.

**v7 bear grain.** Grow ears of grain.

**v8 crop.** Harvest.

**5** What happens when people hear God's word in verses 7 and 18-19?

_____

_____

**6** How do worries, money and other desires choke God's word?

_____

_____

_____

The thorns are worries, money and the desires for other things. These things can seem more important than following Jesus.

**7** What happens when people hear God's word in verses 8 and 20?

_____

_____

_____

Those who are like good soil hear the good news about Jesus, accept it and continue to be changed by it.

## BIBLE WORDS

**Mark 4:13–20**

**v14 the word.** God's word, the good news about Jesus.

**v15 sown.** Planted.

**v15 Satan.** The devil.

**v16 receive.** Take, accept.

**v17 root.** The part of a plant that grows into the soil to collect water.

**v17 persecution.** Opposition, being treated badly because of Jesus.

**v17 fall away.** Stop following Jesus.

**v19 the deceitfulness of wealth.** The false promises of money.

**v19 desires.** Wishes, longings.

**v19 making it unfruitful.** Stopping it from growing fruit/grain.

**8** Which type of soil would you say best describes you?

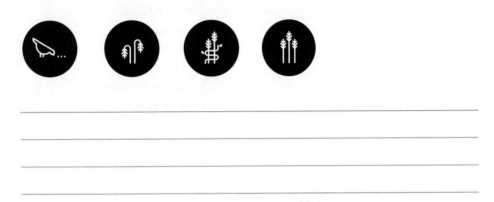

Jesus was clear about the right way to respond to God's word.
"The time has come," he said. "The kingdom of God is near. Repent and believe the good news!"
(Mark 1:15)

That means we must turn from what we know is wrong and trust in what Jesus has done for us when he died on the cross.

# Reading Mark

You may want to read Mark's Gospel during *Christianity Explored*. If you do, these pages will help you. The readings are in short sections, and there is space to write down any thoughts or questions you have. There will be time in the next session to talk about them.

**After Session 1**

Mark 1:1–20

Mark 1:21–39

Mark 1:40 – 2:12

Mark 2:13–22

Mark 2:23 – 3:12

**After Session 2**

Mark 3:13–35

Mark 4:1–20

Mark 4:21–41

Mark 5:1–20

Mark 5:21–43

**After Session 3**

Mark 6:1–29

Mark 6:30–56

Mark 7:1–23

Mark 7:24–37

Mark 8:1–29

**After Session 4**

Mark 8:30 – 9:1

Mark 9:2–32

Mark 9:33–50

Mark 10:1–31

Mark 10:32–52

**After Session 5**

Mark 11:1–19

Mark 11:20–33

Mark 12:1–27

Mark 12:28–44

Mark 13:1–37

**After Session 6**

Mark 14:1–31

Mark 14:32–72

Mark 15:1–20

Mark 15:21–47

Mark 16:1–8

# Keep on exploring...
# www.christianityexplored.org

The *Christianity Explored* website helps you to keep exploring the life and message of Jesus in your own way, at your own pace. It has:

- answers to tough questions.
- a video explaining what Christianity is all about.
- real-life stories from people who've started to follow Jesus.

Many people have found it helps them think about what they believe. We hope you find the same!

**Notes**